CONTENTS

A tri-coloured glazed pottery figurine displaying a 'wild bird' coiffure, with a central roll of hair hanging low over the brow. Height 43cm. Excavated in Xi'an, 1959.

(Endpapers) Tri-colour pottery figure of a seated lady at her toilette. Height 47.3cm. Excavated in Xi'an, 1955.

D0905423

WOMEN OF THE TANG DYNASTY

The Tang dynasty (AD618–907) is often characterized as a Golden Age in Chinese history. Under one of its greatest emperors, Taizong (reigned AD627–649), military conquests extended Chinese domination as far as the Pamirs. A brilliant civilization that found expression in poetry, painting, dance, music and crafts flourished in a rich and powerful empire. Contributing to this intellectual and artistic ferment were the ideas and customs of travellers from other lands, notably Persia, India and Central Asia, who flocked to work or trade or spread their faiths in the imperial capital Chang'an (on the site of the modern city of Xi'an).

Chang'an's affluence and luxury, and the opportunities these created for leisure, were conducive to the development of a refined and sophisticated way of living. Women were not excluded from this civilized lifestyle—indeed they acquired in Tang society an equality and status unprecedented in the history of China up to that time. Those of the upper classes, in particular, and wives and daughters of wealthy merchants were able to take an active part in social life, to walk freely in the streets and to flaunt their femininity. They also pursued such traditionally male activities as riding and playing polo. A fad developed during the middle years of the dynasty when women, led by ladies of the court, took to wearing men's clothes. Princess Taiping, younger sister of the emperor Gaozong, danced for her brother in a man's purple gown, belt and scarf. It is somehow apt that the only female sovereign in Chinese history, Empress Wu Zetian (AD625–706), ruled during the early Tang.

(opposite) A tri-coloured glazed pottery figurine displaying a 'wild bird' coiffure, with a central roll of hair hanging low over the brow. Height 43cm. Excavated in Xi'an, 1959. (above) White jade bracelets set with gold.

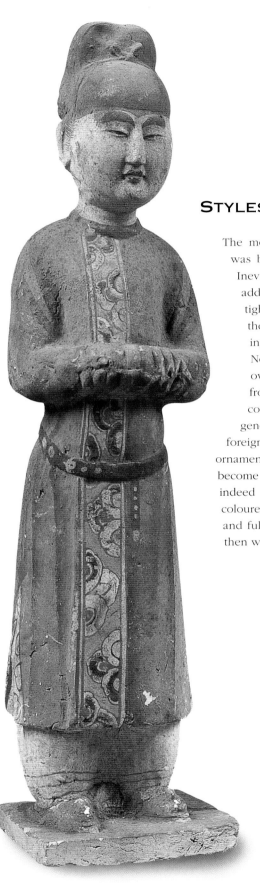

STYLES OF DRESS

The more conventional style of dress for Tang women was based on a bodice or top and ankle-length skirt. Inevitably fashion dictated the refinements and details added to this basic style—the tops would either be tight-fitting or loose, hemlines rose and dropped, and the fabrics used were more or less luxurious, depending on the economic circumstances of the wearer. Nevertheless, three broad trends can be discerned over the period. First there was the style inherited from the previous Sui dynasty (AD581–618), which consisted of short, close-fitting bodices and long skirts, generally in dark colours. Later, clothes modelled on foreign costumes were the rage, and by then more ornamentation, as well as bold and exotic colours, had become popular. In the third phase a more voluptuous, indeed plump, figure came into vogue, and brightly-coloured but loose-fitting garments with high waistlines and full sleeves were preferred. The favourite ornaments then were hairpins.

As the eastern terminus of the Silk Road, Chang'an played host to thousands of foreign travellers. Foreign influence can be seen in some of the fashions shown on these two pottery figurines, who wear front-opening robes over trousers. Accessories included belts with gold or silver fittings, hats and boots.

A maidservant—one of many pottery figurines buried in the tomb of a Tang princess, Yongtai— wearing her hair in two coils on either side of the ears, and in a dress with a décolleté neckline. (opposite) Another example of a figurine displaying a brightly-coloured dress with a high waistline and full sleeves.

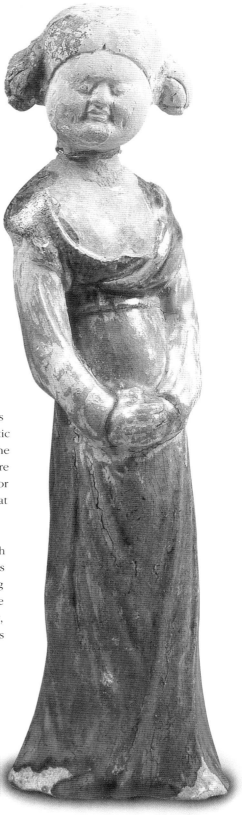

Women in Tang society enjoyed experimenting with ways to enhance their appearance and charms. As time went on the cut of their dresses also became less staid than those of the previous age. Tight, high-collared tops were abandoned in favour of garments with wider collars and even décolleté necklines, inspiring many an erotic reference to the barely covered snow-white breasts in the poems of the day. The trend towards greater exposure could also be observed in hats and veils, originally worn for modesty's sake, which gradually gave way to headgear that showed more and more of the wearer's face.

Descriptions in historical records of garments which belonged to a princess included silk brocade skirts embroidered with motifs of birds and flowers, shimmering with gold thread and coloured feathers. Another fine imperial outfit is a woollen skirt with gold embroidery, thought to have belonged to Empress Wu, which was discovered in the crypt of Famen Temple near Xi'an.

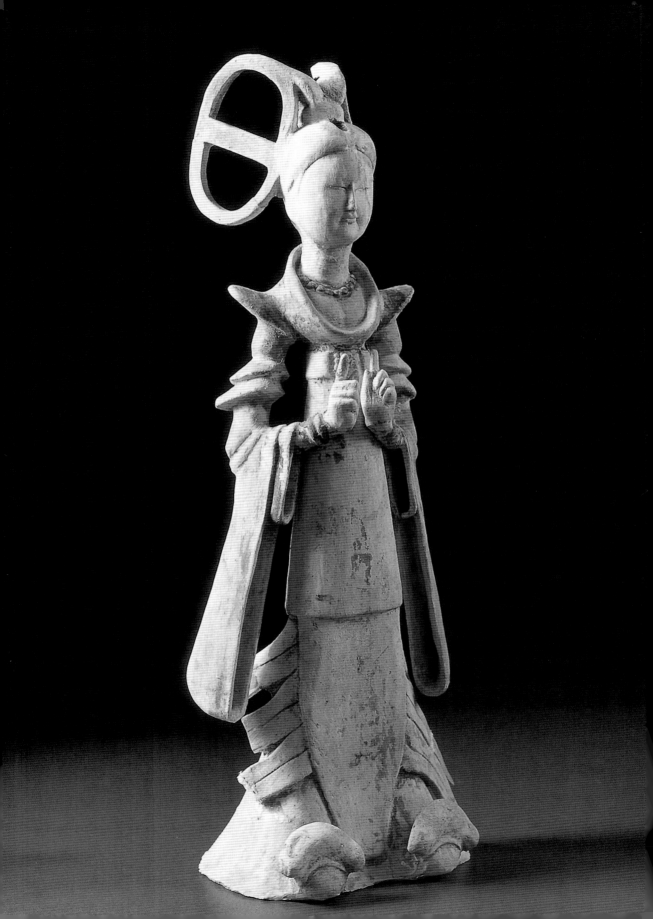

HAIRSTYLES

It was customary to bury earthenware models of servants, horses, buildings and other objects in tombs, to accompany the deceased in their after-life. The most striking feature of the pottery figurines of women is undoubtedly their extraordinary hairstyles. People of ancient China believed that some part of the essence and life force of a human being was contained in the hair. Women traditionally grew their hair long and in the Tang dynasty they wore it in a multitude of different styles, most of them involving plaiting or coiling and piling up the tresses in towering edifices on top of the head. These elaborate coiffures were given delightful names, such as *yunji* (resembling clouds), *luoji* (resembling a spiralling shell), *hudie ji* (resembling the wings of a butterfly), *paojia ji* (a high chignon, with thick bunches forward of the ears) and so on.

To hold up long coils of hair, pins were used. Hairpins could be a *zan*, a single pin with a decorative top; a *chai*, a double-pronged pin with a decorative top; or a *buyao*, a double-pronged pin with a decorative top from which beads dangled. Like jewellery, hairpins made of precious metals and decorated with gems proclaimed the wealth of the wearer, like 'The Salt Merchant's Wife' in the poem by Bai Juyi (AD772–846):

> Growing rich, many gold hair-pins adorn her glossy hair;
> Growing plump, the silver bracelet on her arm is tight.

(above) Examples of silver chai—double-pronged hairpins decorated with bird and peony designs. (opposite) A pottery figurine displaying a spectacular example of both dress and hairstyle.

Tang women also tucked combs in their hair to hold it in place. Combs, too, were often made of gold and silver, as well as jade, horn and shell.

Hair as a beauty feature is celebrated in famous poems, such as 'Song of Eternal Sorrow' by Bai Juyi, which tells the story of Yang Guifei, an imperial concubine. Reputed to be of outstanding beauty, Yang was one of several *femmes fatales* in Chinese history who were held responsible by later generations for the downfall of dynasties. It is said that the Tang emperor Xuanzong, smitten by Yang Guifei, put aside his duties of government to spend time with her.

He had his first sight of her as she emerged from her bath:

> Her hair like a cloud,
> Her face like a flower,
> A gold hair-pin adorning her tresses.
> Behind the warm lotus-flower curtain,
> They took their pleasure in the spring night...

(opposite) Painted pottery figurine with plump figure and one of the many elaborate hairstyles fashionable during the period. (top) The back of a gilt bronze mirror, inlaid with images of four phoenixes trailing ribbons, a design symbolising eternal love. Diameter 22.7cm. (above) Part of a gold comb.

(right) The 'just fallen off a horse look' hairstyle, popularized by the imperial concubine Yang Gufei, on a painted pottery model of a woman with a fashionably plump figure. (below) Gilded silver bracelets.

Yang was allegedly the author of the coiffure known as the 'just fallen off a horse look'—a style she inadvertently created when, after taking a tumble when out riding, the high arrangement of her cloudy tresses came loose on one side. If anything, the delightfully dishevelled state of her hairdo made her look even more beautiful, so it was not surprising that the other palace ladies rushed to copy her.

Such interest in personal adornment was not admired by all, however. A high-ranking government official made so bold as to criticize these elaborate coiffures, describing them as too impractical for ordinary women, and urging the palace ladies to set a less frivolous example. Emperor Taizong angrily riposted: 'Are women in the palace expected to be like bald monks?'

COSMETICS AND MAKE-UP

From very early times women had used cosmetics to supply what nature did not endow. Besides dressing their hair in intricate coiffures and wearing hairpins and jewellery, women in the Tang dynasty had recourse to several types of make-up. They used face powder, of which there were two kinds—rice powder and white lead powder. The latter became more popular and eventually displaced rice powder as a cosmetic. White lead powder was used with rouge, which is thought to have originated from the Xiongnu tribal lands in the northwest. There, in the Yanzhi mountains, thrived a plant from which yellow and red pigments were extracted. The red was used as a dye to produce rouge; this was mixed with a little water before application.

There are many references in Chinese literature to beautiful women's 'moth eyebrows'. Clearly eyebrows were also considered a feature of beauty and much plucking and painting went on to enhance their attractiveness. Emperor Han Wudi (reigned 140–86 BC) liked his concubines to have eyebrows rising to meet at the centre of the forehead, a fashion dubbed *ba-zimei*, after the Chinese character for eight, 八. In the Three Kingdoms period (AD220–265), when powerful regional warlords clashed to gain control of China, one of the contenders, Cao Cao, had a preference for long dark eyebrows on his women. Emperor Yangdi of the Sui, the short-lived dynasty that preceded the Tang, acquired large supplies of

(above) Gold cosmetic case. (opposite) Painted pottery figure of a woman holding a mirror.

a substance from Persia that was used to draw eyebrows for his wife and concubines. The infatuated Xuanzong, during a period of exile from the capital while a rebellion raged in the north of the empire, had an artist draw for him a picture of ten eyebrow styles, no doubt to recall 'she with the moth-like eyebrows'— Yang Guifei, who had been killed by his mutinous troops on the journey into exile.

Cosmetics were applied to other parts of the face. Coloured foreheads were considered extremely chic at one time. Buddha statues were conventionally made with golden foreheads, and this inspired a fashion of decorating the skin above the eyebrows, either by painting it yellow or by sticking on a yellow patch cut out in the shape of a flower. A princess of the Southern dynasty is credited with originating this practice. It seems she was resting on a balcony in the Nanjing palace one day when a blossom from a nearby plum tree was blown onto her forehead. The outline of the petals remained there for three days, inspiring a host of imitators who resorted to other materials such as gold leaf, fish bones, mother-of-pearl and oyster shell, so that not only plum blossom patterns but outlines of birds and fish also began appearing over their brows.

A plum blossom in gold leaf, once used as a forehead decoration. It would have been stuck to the centre of the brow with glue.

Besides decorating their foreheads, Tang women also painted crescent-shaped red marks on their temples and, of course, applied colour to their lips. Indeed, lipsticks made a very early appearance in China, and the 'cherry mouth' was admired and celebrated in verse by Bai Juyi.

Cloud-shaped silver box embossed with a design of honeysuckle and parrots.

Jade powder compact, with carved mandarin ducks and lotus motif.

As in 18th-century Europe, imitation beauty spots were in vogue, but in China the appearance of the first one was said to have been the result of an accident. This happened during the Three Kingdoms period. A kinsman of the royal Wu clan, intoxicated after a heavy night of drinking, inadvertently struck his wife with a jade sceptre. A physician, summoned to treat her wound, concocted an ointment of otter bone marrow, ground jade and ground amber. This guaranteed that the wound would leave no scar, he assured the distraught husband. But the ointment contained a little too much amber, and this left the lady with a red spot where a dimple might be. Curiously, this made her more alluring, to the delight of the husband and the fury of his concubines.

By the Tang dynasty, much more deliberation was going into the preparation of beauty spots, which could be variously shaped (apricot-shaped and soya-bean-shaped ones were popular) and were chosen to match the clothes and hairstyles being worn. Generally the spots were made by dotting the cheek with rouge, but they could also be made of gold foil or kingfisher feather.

Silver box with flower and foliage design.

TANG WOMEN'S LOVE OF GOLD AND SILVER

All these methods of personal adornment led, inevitably, to a proliferation of paraphernalia for the dressing table, such as bronze mirrors, gold and silver receptacles for cosmetics, powder boxes and containers for potpourri.

Gold and silver have always had an allure for women, not just in the Tang. Objects made in these precious metals were generally the most prestigious and acceptable gifts from a father, husband or master. It was during the Tang, however, that metalworking skills attained the level of art. From the gold and silver relics of the period, it is clear that the artist-craftsmen were beginning to place as much emphasis on aesthetics as on function. Boxes for cosmetics, pieces of jewellery, and even everyday articles for the house were all made with the aim of creating shapes and styles that were not only useful but also attractive.

Decorative techniques included embossing, engraving, filigree and openwork. The designs reveal many influences; the bird and foliage motif, for example, was adopted by Chinese craftsmen from the Middle East. Auspicious feminine symbols, notably grapes and phoenixes (representing fertility and love respectively), embellished articles used by women such as mirrors. Mirrors made during the Tang show that the composition of bronze at the time was 70% copper, 25% tin and 5% lead. One side of the mirror was highly polished to provide a reflective surface; the reverse was usually decorated.

Sea beast and grapes motif on a bronze mirror.

Mirror back, with a motif known as 'palace of the moon'. The moon, phoenix and grapes, with their traditional feminine associations, were symbols of love and fertility.

Gilded silver basket decorated with geese in flight. Height 17.8cm, diameter 16.1cm. Excavated from the crypt of Famen Temple, Fufeng, Shaanxi, 1987.

Metalwork Techniques

Xi'an in Shaanxi has a rich heritage of metal relics from the Tang dynasty, when it was the site of the imperial capital, Chang'an. Two of the three largest caches of Tang gold and silver treasures ever unearthed were found in the province: the first in 1970 at Hejia village, and the second beneath the Famen Temple in Fufeng County, which was discovered in 1987. (The third was excavated in 1982 at Dingmaoqiao, Dantu, in Jiangsu Province.)

The first gold articles in China were made during the Shang dynasty (16th–11th centuries BC). By the Tang dynasty some 17 centuries later, metalworking had developed into a sophisticated craft. Both the prosperity of the age and the rise in gold production contributed to this development. The techniques used had their origins in the bronzeware manufacture of the Western and Eastern Han dynasties (206BC–AD8 and AD25–220). Later the popularity of bronze declined, although the material continued to be used in the manufacture of mirrors.

Gold and silver wares in the Tang were usually cast rather than turned and beaten, and their surfaces were chased or inlaid with mother of pearl or precious stones. Openwork was another technique, most appealingly employed in the manufacture of *xiangnang* (ball-shaped censers), two of which were discovered in the Famen Temple. Each censer consists of a hollow ball on a chain, with a bowl suspended on a circular axis inside. No matter how the censer was swung, the interior bowl would not spill its aromatic herbs or burning incense. To create one, the gold- or silversmith would have beaten his metal into a ball around 4.5 centimetres in diameter before hollowing it out. The material was then pierced to create the openwork decoration, which often depicted grapes or birds in flight.

Not surprisingly, gold and silver articles were possessed only by the richest echelons of Tang society—the imperial family, the nobility, and well-patronised temples. A woman of refinement or one from a wealthy family could afford to be fastidious. She would order her ladies in waiting to carry censers, to scent a room or space she occupied. Censers were also hung on chariots and sedans and used at burials. Emperor Xuanzong, returning from exile in Sichuan, had the body of his beloved Yang Guifei exhumed so that she could be re-buried in a more appropriate grave. Her corpse and clothing had already begun to decay, but the heavy scent from numerous *xiangnang* masked the unpleasant smell. Princess Tongqiang, Yizong's daughter, hung censers burning imported incense from the four corners of her sedan chair. Some noblewomen put Buddhist sutras in their *xiangnang* to ward off evil.

The malleability of gold means that one gramme of pure gold can be stretched into filigree 0.00434 millimetres in diameter and 3,500 metres in length. A magnificent example of the goldsmith's elaborate workmanship is shown by the flowers-and-clouds decoration on the gold cup illustrated.

(top and opposite) Gilded silver xiangnang *(incense burner) decorated with birds in flight and grapes. Diameter 4.5cm. (bottom) Gold cup decorated with flowers and clouds. Height 5.9cm, diameter 6.8cm. Both excavated from Hejia village, Xi'an, 1970.*

DESIGNS

Many of the gold and silver objects from the Tang show a foreign influence in their design, decoration and method of manufacture, an influence that was spread to China by merchants from west and central Asia via the Silk Road.

The strongest design influence on early and mid-Tang gold and silverware came from Sute in central Asia. The octagonal silver cup decorated with flowers and birds exhibits a Sute shape and ornamentation.

Gradually gold and silverware began to acquire Chinese characteristics. For a time hybrid wares were produced. The silver goblet with a hunting design has a shape that bears Byzantine traces, but its decoration is Chinese. An octagonal, petal-shaped silver cup

Silver goblet with a hunting design. Height 7cm, diameter 5.9cm.
Excavated from Hejia village, Xi'an, 1970.

Octagonal silver cup decorated with flowers and birds.
Height 6.1cm, diameter 6.8cm. Excavated in Xi'an, 1982.

depicting women and hunting combines Sute and Chinese features. Each petal depicts a scene, four showing men and four of women. The men are on horseback, poised to shoot their arrows. In contrast, the women look relaxed as they groom themselves, comb their hair and play with babies. The inside of the cup is also decorated with a pattern of fish and aquatic plants. When the cup is filled with water, it is supposed to resemble a pond.

Octagonal, petal-shaped gilded silver cup
depicting women and hunting.
Height 5.1cm, diameter 9.1cm. Excavated
from Hejia village, Xi'an, 1970.

Gold drinking vessel with mojie *design. Height 3.5cm, diameter 13.1cm. Excavated in Xi'an, 1983.*

A gold drinking vessel with *mojie* design is one example of a Chinese vessel with decoration showing Indian influence. In the centre of the inside base of the cup is the *mojie*, a mythical creature with a long nose, sharp teeth, and a fish's body and tail, which was respected as the spirit of rivers and the root of all life. It was featured in sutras brought to China during the Eastern Jin dynasty (AD317–420). From then on, many *mojie* designs were used on gold and silver objects.

In the late Tang era, when there was a backlash against Buddhism, the shape and design of gold and silverware assumed entirely Chinese characteristics, as shown by the lotus leaf-shaped silver cup with the two-fish design.

The gold bowl patterned with lotus petals is an example of fretwork where two layers of the metal beaten into the shape of lotus petals form the main ornamental feature. The top layer of petals is adorned with animal motifs: sika, rabbit, river deer, parrot and mandarin duck. The second layer is decorated with the outlines of honeysuckle, while the inside of the bowl is etched with thousands of little fish, which symbolize children and happiness. In another example featuring the lotus, the overlapping leaves on the gilded silver bowl look most realistic because of the thinness of the metal.

(above) Gold bowl decorated with animals and birds. Height 5.5cm, diameter 13.7cm. Excavated from Hejia village, Xi'an, 1970.
(right) Gilded silver bowl with overlapping lotus leaf pattern. Height 8cm, diameter 16cm. Excavated from the crypt of Famen Temple, Fufeng, Shaanxi, 1987.

(opposite page, top) Gilded silver drinking vessel decorated with twin fish, flowers and leaves. (bottom) Lotus leaf-shaped silver bowl decorated with sea creatures.

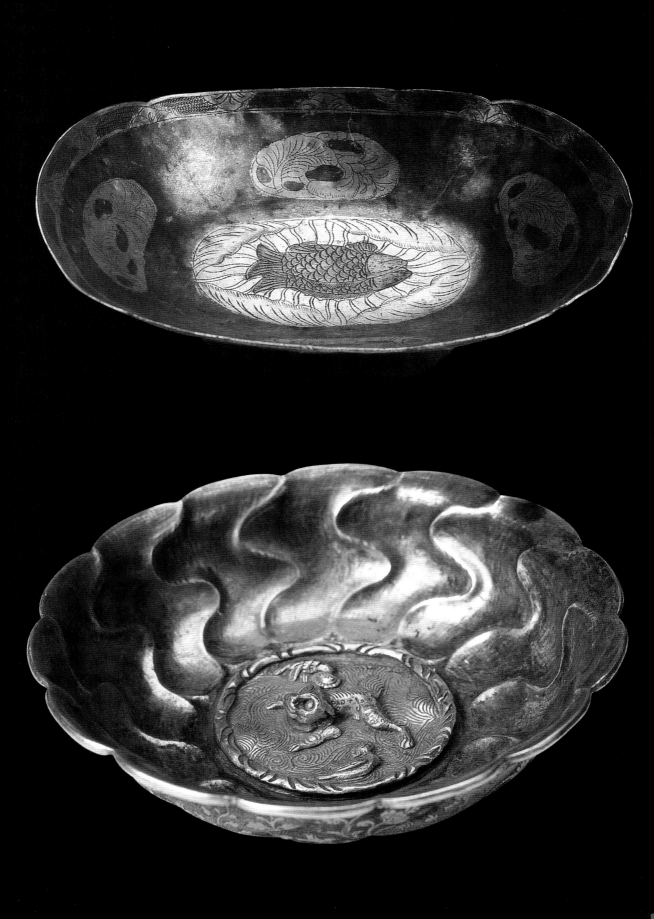

RELICS FROM THE PALACE

Gold basin.
Height 6.5cm, diameter 28.6cm.
Excavated from Hejia village,
Xi'an, 1970.

Articles and ornaments were manufactured in gold and silver for everyday use in the imperial palace and as ritual vessels in temples. Gold was even taken internally as an elixir by those in search of a long life.

The gold basin illustrated is the only surviving example of its kind from the Tang dynasty. Others were doubtless stolen from tombs, melted down and reworked. This basin was hammered into shape by hand, then polished, probably with the aid of some kind of rudimentary tool, to produce its fine surface sheen. The poet Wang Jian (c. 767–830), in *Palace*, gives a hint as to its use:

> The emperor arrived and all the maids
> Washed their faces and put on make-up.

Gold basins also had ceremonial uses. Whether it was the empress or an imperial concubine who gave birth, the arrival of a baby was a happy event. When the child was three days old, a ceremonial washing in a gold basin was held. The poet Zhang E, in *Three Days in Qiwang's Home*, wrote: 'The imperial concubine had a baby girl who started to cry. After washing in a gold basin, she was wrapped in an embroidered sheet...'

Emperors often gave gifts in gold and silver to courtiers, ministers, local officials and concubines as tokens of favour. At the winter solstice, the emperor would grant silver cosmetic boxes to his maids. The exquisitely-made silver box illustrated was probably a gift from an emperor.

Silver box decorated with interwoven flowers.
Excavated from Hejia village, Xi'an, 1970.

The Tang palace was normally home to over 3,000 beautiful women, but the emperor never noticed more than a lucky few. Vying for the emperor's favour, his concubines would throw gold coins to see whose turn it was to please him. Under the Tang emperor Xuanzong, gold coins known as Kaiyuan (the name denoting his reign) were used for this game. They bore the characters *Kai Yuan Tong Bao*, and were modelled on copper coins, the legal tender of the time.

Despite all the attention, however, Xuanzong's best-loved concubine remained Yang Guifei. After her arrival at the palace, the coin-tossing game stopped.

Gold and silver coins were also issued to celebrate the birth of babies to imperial concubines. One of the most bizarre of such coin issues was to mark the adoption of An Lushan by Yang Guifei. General An, only 15 years younger than Yang, was rumoured to be her lover rather than her adopted son.

Silver plates were made in several different shapes. The plate with a turtle design at its centre—a Sute feature—is in the shape of a peach. The fruit is said to have originated in China. Peach stones dating back to the late Shang dynasty, at least 3,000 years old, have been excavated at Taixi in Gaocheng County, Hebei Province.

There were several kinds of peach, the most popular being the *xiwangmu*. People believed that by eating the fruit they could shake off fatigue, while Taoists regarded the peach as a symbol of longevity. Another auspicious symbol of longevity is the turtle.

*Gold **Kaiyuan** coin.*
Diameter 2.3cm.
Excavated from
Hejia village,
Xi'an, 1970.

Gilded silver plate decorated with a turtle.
Diameter 12.3cm. Excavated from
Hejia village, Xi'an, 1970.

Gilded silver plates decorated with a phoenix (left) and flying ox (right).
Diameter 15.3cm. Both excavated from Hejia village, Xi'an, 1970.

Legend has it that a Taoist presented a small gold turtle to Xuanzong and told him that by keeping the talisman he could enjoy a long life without encountering evil or disaster.

The silver plate with the gilded turtle is one of five such plates excavated in Hejia village. The other four are equally distinctive: there is one in the shape of two peaches decorated with a pair of foxes; another shows a flying ox; the third is a round plate adorned with a pattern of rocks and flowers; and the fourth, a diamond-shaped plate, carries a design of phoenixes. All five silver plates typify Chinese design and decoration.

Other favourite motifs included mandarin ducks and climbing plants, which stand out in the *man di zhuang* (all-over decoration) of the gold pot illustrated opposite.

The rarity, lustre and beauty of gold and silver were much prized by Tang rulers. The durability of these precious metals has meant that the wealth of ornaments they commissioned for their empresses and concubines, as well as the articles for use in the palace, still bear testimony to a glorious culture that continue to astonish and fascinate.

Gold pot decorated with mandarin ducks and climbing plants.
Height 21cm, diameter 11cm. Excavated at Xianyang, Shaanxi, 1969.

Major Museums of Xi'an and Shaanxi Province

The province of Shaanxi is the geographical and historical heartland of China. Encompassing 20,000 square kilometres of fertile land and drained by the Yellow River and its tributaries, it was imperial China's political, economic and cultural centre for more than a millennium. The modern city of Xi'an stands near the site of Chang'an, the capital of China's first empire. Altogether 13 dynasties located their capitals here. The Zhou, Qin, Han, Sui and Tang dynasties, in particular, left thousands of relics, dating from around 1000BC to AD900, in Xi'an and the surrounding countryside. This rich cultural heritage is displayed in more than 70 museums in the province. Collections include magnificent bronzes; terracotta warriors and horses; stone sculptures; inscribed stone tablets; gold, silver and jade artefacts; murals and porcelain. The map opposite shows the locations of nine major museums that exhibit a broad representation of Shaanxi's cultural legacy.

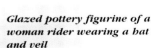

Glazed pottery figurine of a woman rider wearing a hat and veil